THE LITTLE BOOKLET ON:

DESIGN THINKING

An Introduction

2nd Edition

MONIKA HESTAD - ANDERS GROENLI - SILVIA RIGONI

BRANDVALLEY PUBLICATIONS

For Viktor

The Little Booklet on Design Thinking: An Introduction
2nd Edition 2017
1st Edition 2013

This book is part of the series 'The Little Booklet on...'
Published by Brand Valley Publications
© Brand Valley Design Ltd, London 2017
All rights reserved.

Layout: Marianne Hollum Lydersen
Illustrations: Silvia Rigoni

Brand Valley Design Ltd
34B York Way
London, N1 9AB
United Kingdom

Brand Valley AS
publications@brandvalley.uk
www.brandvalley.uk

ISBN 978-1-912220-01-4

CONTENTS

Too often we are charging ahead to find answers and solutions without checking that finding the answer would actually make a difference.*

* Dr Bettina von Stamm

FOREWORD

By Dr Bettina von Stamm, founder and Director of the Innovation Leadership Forum

I am absolutely delighted to have been asked to write the foreword to this second edition of *The Little Booklet on Design Thinking*. Why? We are living in times that are faster-moving and more complex than ever before. The constant change is a consequence of the possibilities to make connections, to combine different bits of knowledge, and do so with a speed that was never possible before. According to Cisco (2016), global Internet traffic has risen from 100 GB per day in 1992 to 100 GB per second in 2002 to 20,235 GB per second in 2015.

The constant change, connectivity and convergence are responsible for the increasing complexity we have to face – a complexity that arises from a large number of factors interacting in non-linear, non-predictable ways. So, as the systems of which we are part are changing constantly around us, we ourselves also need to adapt, constantly re-learning how to negotiate our world, how to find our way. And that is where design thinking comes in.

For me, four aspects are key to design thinking:
1.   It is human-centred. It puts users or customers at the centre of attention, trying to understand them and their needs. This is done in a particular context and through observation and investigation of all facets that are relevant to the

challenge in question.

2. Prototyping and other forms of visualisation are key aspects. It can be difficult to describe and communicate something that does not (yet) exist. Making things visual through drawings, prototypes and animations helps people understand and engage with a new proposition.

3. Participation of people from diverse backgrounds and drawing on varied input and perspectives are essential. This links back to the 'context' and 'all facets' mentioned in the first point: design thinking takes a holistic approach to a problem or a challenge. It investigates the context and all stakeholders in order to come up with a solution.

4. It is a journey where divergent phases alternate with convergent phases, and it is iterative, meaning that phases where we try to open up and identify many possibilities and opportunities alternate with phases where we try to narrow our options down as much as possible.

Design thinking – and innovation – are about opening up possibilities and identifying opportunities to then iterate the process throughout the different stages of the innovation process.

Too often we are charging ahead to find answers and solutions without checking that finding the answer would actually make a difference. When talking to a manager at Unilever about the environmental sustainability of tea bags, he pointed out:

'We can put as much effort as we like into improving the footprint of individual tea bags, what really would make a

*difference to the footprint of the UK's beloved cup of tea is
people boiling only as much water as they need.'*

In our drive for speed and results, we tend to forget to question
whether we have truly identified the underlying cause, or only
one of the symptoms.

Dr Bettina von Stamm

WHY THIS BOOKLET?

Learn design thinking through a creative and engaging development process.

In 2013, when we first published *The Little Booklet on Design Thinking*, the concept of design thinking was a buzz word. Now the concept 'design thinking' has matured and evolved into something beyond the buzz, proving its worth in areas of policy making, of developing new products and services and new business models. Because design thinking is evolving, it was time to revisit this booklet and update it with new and fresh content. The version you have in your hands is not a complete redesign, but a facelift to engage with the growing development of design thinking.

Harvard Business Review has published several articles on the topic, with its September 2015 cover highlighting that design is increasingly helping to shape companies' overall strategy and management (HBR, 2015) particularly for those challenges that do not have a simple solution design and that could benefit from design thinking (Neumeier, 2009). For example, how can you design services and products that are fitted both for the organisational needs as well as for the audience they are supposed to serve. How can you design products and services that are relevant for the market as well as flexible and adaptable for future changes? How can employees have meaningful jobs while retaining good salaries and benefits?

A popular explanation of design thinking is that it is a process in phases that starts with observing human beings and identifying needs, developing prototypes and thereby testing these (HBR, 2015). We believe that mastering design thinking is not about learning one method or formula, but about attaining an attitude about continuous improvement and learning. The insight on continuous improvement is key to solving the challenges we are faced with. People are put at the centre of attention, and the goal of the improvement is therefore to increase the benefit the involved individuals attain when using the solution. One learns what the solution should be through exploring the surroundings, and then develops and tests different ideas continuously through the entire process. Design thinking is a holistic approach to development that is about identifying and exploring possibilities. Designers have a toolbox with methods that can help in this work.

In order to implement design thinking in organisations, managers should not only employ designers, but dare to engage with their surroundings using an approach similar to the way a designer would tackle a challenge. This might include taking on the tasks of an employee for a couple of days in order to experience the challenges of this part of the organisation, or explaining strategies by visualising a scenario through visual aids such as LEGO bricks. If you really want an organisation that is driven by design thinking, managers also need to inspire others to embrace the attitude about continuous improvement, and give employees an opportunity to explore, develop and try out new solutions within their areas.

How can people with a non-design background quickly acquire these skills and this way of thinking? The school system has a tendency to emphasise analytical thinking through writing or discussing texts (Robinson, 2006). The acquisition of even the simplest design skills can therefore become a challenge after years of text-based work. Someone in their forties might be terrified by the mere thought of having to visualise something through a drawing, although drawing might have been their preferred way of expression before they learned how to write longer texts. So let's face it: it will take time to change ways of working towards developing a design approach to challenges – but it is possible!

Design thinking is deeply rooted in what the philosopher Donald Schön identified as 'thinking in action' (2011 [1959]). In this booklet, we will introduce a step-by-step process that allows groups to get an idea of what a design approach might be. Through this process it is possible to learn design thinking by performing collaborative tasks. The key to becoming a design thinker is to understand the process and the principles behind it.

The process and the principles have been developed over several years, and have been refined by engaging with industry and by interacting with students from across the world at Central Saint Martins, University of the Arts London since 2009. The process is designed as an interactive experience, as we believe this is how design thinking is best learned. Design thinking cannot be studied solely by reading a book; in addition to reading, it has to be experienced through doing.

Enjoy!

USED BY

Users of the first edition of this booklet range from public sector managers to large and small businesses and university students. Dr Bettina von Stamm, who provided the foreword to this edition, challenged us to design a one-and-a-half-day seminar for her Innovation Leadership Forum Networking Group. This was held at the Google Campus in London in November 2012. The group consisted of 40 delegates from various innovation labs in large corporations across numerous sectors, from finance and IT to consumer goods. The participants came from a variety of backgrounds where the majority were not designers. The seminar followed a step-by-step process similar to this booklet. As so often when it comes to design and innovation, direct impact is difficult to measure. However, Bettina shared that workshop participants kept referring to the learning outcome, and seemed to have integrated it into their ways of thinking and acting.

The Scottish Government's Strategy Unit ran a one-day workshop solely for a group of public sector managers based on the process outlined in the booklet. They developed their own scenario, relevant for managers in the public sector.

Their feedback was that:

'The Scottish Government puts people's lived experience at the heart of policy making; we can't achieve that without deepening trust and understanding in our relationships. We have to start with the right attitude, and design thinking gives us ways to genuinely engage with people to ensure they shape public policy and services. The Little Booklet on Design Thinking has contributed to the Scottish Government

by helping us put the principles of engagement, empathy and trust at the heart of our policy making. It's a clear, fun and practical way of putting those principles into action.'

They further said that this helped them to introduce design thinking in an efficient way. By developing a scenario of their own and adapting the process to this scenario, they managed to make it relevant for public sector managers.

The booklet has been used as an eye-opener tool in a teaching situation at Lund University in Sweden. Senior Lecturer Elin Olander at the School of Design uses the booklet in a course on design methodology for mechanical engineering students. She introduced the principles listed in the booklet in order to open up the students' eyes. The engineering students are already excellent and effective problem solvers when employing analytic tools. However, they have less experience in the intuitive approach to problem solving. Design thinking bridges analytic and intuitive mindsets, and the principles of this booklet therefore served to expand the students' approach to developing solutions.

Participants who have used this process have particularly highlighted the importance of introducing more creative thinking into daily life. Users of the first edition of the booklet have mentioned that the innovation departments in their organisations can sometimes be too focused on analysis, and that a process such as the one we describe makes it easier to open up to alternative ways of thinking.

We found that a structured process that emphasises creativity can challenge existing practices. Finally, the most important lesson from the participants who tested this process is that by having fun, we work more efficiently.

Design thinking is reflection through action.
This means that the approach and solution to the
challenge emerge while working.*

---

*Based on the American philosopher and organisational learning researcher Donald
Schön's observations of how designers go about their work.

A LEARNING PROCESS

How to use the booklet.

Designers have a holistic approach to development, where a significant aspect is that the process and the ideas are developed during practice. This can be experienced as something different than others' approach to development work. This booklet has therefore sought to make design thinking more concrete through the introduction of a step-by-step process. This follows guiding principles which mirror a general design process. We encourage readers to use the process in an active manner, and to test it. The readers can then use the principles described on page 89 to reflect on what lies behind the process.

The step-by-step process in this booklet can be used in various contexts and for various purposes:

To learn about design thinking

To solve specific problems

To inspire new processes through design thinking

To develop new products or services from scratch

To teach others about design thinking

BRIEF DESCRIPTION OF THE PROCESS

The step-by-step process in this booklet has been developed as a learning experience to give a taste of how a design process can develop.

A design process evolves through different stages. It often starts with an exploration stage, where the goal is to understand the context of the challenge at hand and who to involve. When one has gained an overview of the challenge, and it has been defined, the process enters into an ideation stage. First a range of ideas are generated. Then one or more ideas are developed for further testing and concept development. The concept is developed to a prototype and evaluated. If satisfied with the result, the solution is implemented. A process driven by a desire for continuous improvement often continues after you have tested the solution. Through every exploration, development and testing, you will come closer to the core of the challenge. In the chapter 'Thoughts on the process' you can read more about how it relates to a real design process.

The step-by-step process in this booklet is simplified to allow group collaboration over a short period of time. The intention of this process is not that is should solve all problems, but that it can be a useful introduction.

The process involves:

Immersion
Ideation
Concept development
Prototyping

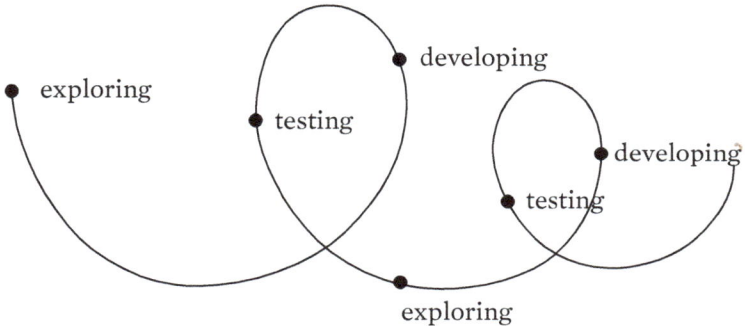

Immersion: In the first stage, it will be important to immerse yourself in the context to understand what you are dealing with. In order to do so, you and the design team will need to conduct research. In this stage it will be important to identify potential needs, desires and challenges.

To simplify this in this booklet, we chose to emphasise the importance of imagination. Once immersed in the context, designers are encouraged to reframe the challenge to examine whether there is something beyond the visible challenge.

Ideation: When the nature of the challenge has been identified and phrased as an opportunity, the team is ready to embark on ideas. The ideation stage explores and opens up needs that have been identified in the immersion stage so that they can be developed into a wide range of potential solutions. This stage leads to identifying ideas that could be interesting to develop further.

Concept development: In this stage, the idea is developed further into a concept. An important aspect of this stage is to make the concept as robust as possible. Is it viable from a business point of view? Is it technologically feasible? And is it what people desire?

Prototyping: Prototyping requires the developer to make all the decisions necessary in order to make the project as real as possible. Prototyping will therefore help the discussion to change from 'This could be ...' to 'This is ...'. An important part of prototyping is testing. Once that testing is complete, you will know whether you should go forward, or whether you need to redesign your solution.

Design thinking combines analytical and intuitive mindsets and allows the involvement of all stakeholders in a co-operative activity. The aim of this co-operation is to provide a joint journey towards a solid solution.*

* Inspired by Roger Martin (2009).

GETTING STARTED

A few tips to kick off the process.

The step-by-step process works best when you are several people working together. It can be beneficial to include participants with diverse backgrounds. This can lead to new perspectives when ideas are explored. If you organise a collaborative project, there are some tips we would like to share with you:

Planning the experience

When running the workshop as a seminar, the whole experience must be planned, from the delegates' arrival to their leaving. To set the tone and help the participants relax, it is important to plan how the activities of the day should be introduced. In addition to the steps, it is recommended to include a welcome pack, introduction and debriefing session (Sims, 2006). It can also be useful to prepare a couple of off-the-shelf exercises to use when the energy is low (before and after the lunch break, for instance). As the creativity and the joy of development take over, it is also important to allow time for reflection in between the tasks or stages if the goal is that the participants should learn about design thinking.

Environment

In order for the group to collaborate effectively, it is important to create an environment of openness and sharing. A key part of this facilitation will involve organising the space where the workshop takes place. If possible, the groups should work in a seating arrangement where no one is allowed to start with a dominant role (e.g. by using a round table). You will also need to consider access to water, snacks and energisers. These will be important to maintain motivation throughout the tasks.

Ground rules

When working in the groups, it is also important to create a dynamic where the decisions made are not always a compromise, but are based on the recognition of a strong concept. To achieve this, it will be important to define a few ground rules before embarking upon this journey into design thinking. An aspect of defining these will involve structuring the group. Group work performs better if there is a facilitator. Other roles vital to the group dynamic are:

A timekeeper

A facilitator

A motivator

Other rules could cover how strictly the group should follow time limits, when it needs to conclude, how to resolve conflicts, how to document the ideas, and whether its decisions need to be based on consensus. If these rules are defined before starting, the participants can refer to them during the process. This can prevent conflicts that might arise or one person dominating the discussion, particularly when deciding which ideas to pursue.

Time management

Time management is necessary, as the participants will most likely need to complete the workshop by a particular time. Group members will need to go through all the stages, and will in most cases find that they are pressed for time in completing each of the tasks. They will probably need a gentle push to go forward to the next stage.

It is important to keep in mind that a workshop has its limitations. Incubation is an essential part of the process, as ideas take time to develop.

Workshops are useful to generate ideas and to share insights, as well as to make a few decisions. Workshops are also useful for educational purposes and as a shared space where different stakeholders can develop a shared understanding. After the workshop, it is necessary to take time and look back at what has been developed, criticise it and develop it further. This is an essential part of the iterations.

Tools

Tools in a workshop context include matrices, methods or similar aids that are introduced to assist the thinking process or to structure the work. Sometimes, you may find that the tool is not perfect for what you are working on and therefore needs to be modified; other times, you may find that working on a blank sheet of paper is more helpful than a particular tool.

The tools suggested in this booklet are gathered from multiple sources, and in some cases have been developed by us. A resource list that could help you plan is presented on page 95.

Recommended materials

The following materials are recommended for this process:

**A4 or A3 sheets of paper
(US: Letter- or Ledger-sized paper)**

Sticky notes

Markers, pens or pencils

Material for prototyping: cardboard, boxes, Blu Tack, sticky tape, coloured paper etc.

Prepared tools to aid the process. These can be downloaded as templates from: www.brandvalley.co.uk/resources

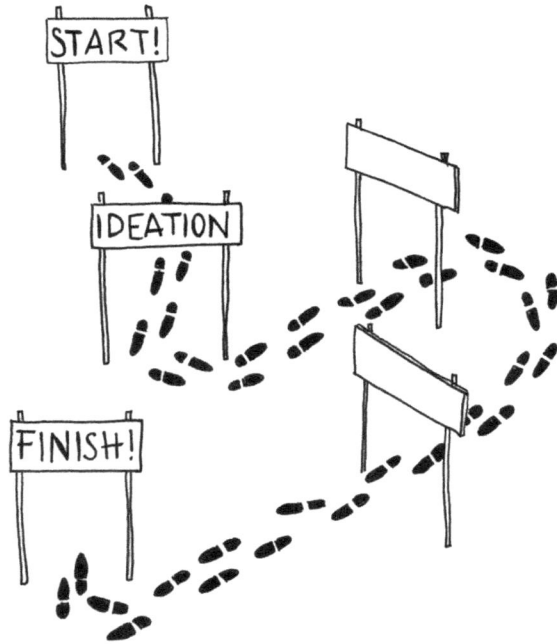

THE STEP-BY-STEP PROCESS

The process is presented as a series of verbal and visual tasks.

The tasks provide a natural progression that facilitates the development of your ideas. You can approach the use of these tasks in several ways:

As an exercise with pen and paper on your own

As a collaborative tabletop exercise with pen and paper

As a full workshop with various visual aids

STAGE 1

IMMERSION

Immerse yourself in the context that the project is part of and identify possible opportunities. Get to know the users.

TASK 1.1

IDENTIFY YOUR USER

To get started, you need to select the area you are going to examine. This can be your own area of work or an area you have been asked to look at. In this area, identify a concrete challenge or a question you have.

Identify a person you would like to develop a new solution for. This could be a target customer for your company, an internal stakeholder in your organisation, or you could choose someone in the Family Tree tool (described on the following page) as your starting point.

> TIP: If you have chosen a real person, you should talk to or observe this person to find out more about how a new solution can help them.

What is the challenge? _____

_____

_____

_____

Who is the chosen person?_____

_____

_____

_____

What do you know about the person? _____

_____

_____

_____

Why did you choose this person? _____

_____

_____

_____

TIP: It is important to understand that you need not see the solutions at this stage. You can identify any subject you want to approach. The challenge identified could be an opportunity you would like to examine, or a question you have. If you see many challenges that need to be addressed, you can write all of them down, which might make it easier to choose one for this task.

Tool: **Meet the Willburns**

Below, we have drawn an imaginary family, the Willburns. Feel free to use any of these characters as your 'user', or use this example to draw up your own family tree (can also be based on needs at work or another place).

82 YEARS OLD
GREAT - GRANDMOTHER
LIVES ALONE 20 MIN AWAY FROM HER FAMILY

INDEPENDENT

HAS HELP FROM THE LOCAL SERVICES ONCE A WEEK

ACTIVE SOCIAL LIFE

USES A READING AID

62 YEARS OLD

ACTIVE AND EXTROVERT

WORKS IN THE ART FIELD

PART OF THE ART COMMUNITY

INJURED HER HAND WHILE GARDENING

ENJOYS SPENDING TIME WITH HER GRANDDAUGHTER

29 YEARS OLD
SINGLE FATHER

WORKS IN THE TECHNOLOGY INDUSTRY

HAS LITTLE TIME FOR HOBBIES

DREAD TAKING PUBLIC TRANSPORT WITH HIS ACTIVE DAUGHTER

4 YEARS OLD
JUST STARTED HER FOUNDATION YEAR

LEARNING TO READ

RAPIDLY BECOMING MORE INDEPENDENT

LOVES PLAYING HIDE AND SEEK

LOVES HER GRANDMOTHER

TASK 1.2

BRAINSTORM DRIVERS OF CHANGE

Think about what is happening today that is changing society. Are there, for example, any political changes or changes in the legislation that affect the challenge you have identified in Task 1.1?

Brainstorm and identify relevant 'drivers of change' that you think might have a major impact on your challenge. In this task, it is useful to structure the brainstorming through a PESTEL (Political, Economic, Social, Technological, Environmental, Legal) tool. Identify at least five developments that you think will affect the challenge and the user you identified in Task 1.1.

TIP: The developments that create changes in society are called 'drivers of change'. The website www.driversofchange.com provides several trends and questions that can help you to identify PESTEL drivers.

_____
_____
_____
_____
_____
_____
_____
_____
_____
_____
_____
_____
_____
_____
_____
_____
_____
_____
_____
_____
_____

TIP: Use PESTEL to identify drivers of change. This can, for example, be new political leadership or increased use of social media. A significant event or trend can influence across categories.

Tool: **PESTEL**

PESTEL	Jot down keywords on trends and events that may be significant:
POLITICAL	
ECONOMIC	
SOCIAL	
TECHNOLOGICAL	
ENVIRONMENTAL	
LEGAL	

TASK 1.2

SCENARIO BUILDING

The aim of this task is to develop three future scenarios.

Use the 'drivers of change' identified in Task 1.2, and imagine how these events and trends may evolve over the next five years.

Start with the person you have worked on so far, and describe further how the trends can affect the person you are developing a solution for.

Merge insights to arrive at scenarios that look at both individual developments and developments in society. These could cover the spectrum from worst to best case.

> TIP: When developing the future scenarios, be as specific as possible. Identify interests, hobbies, work styles, lifestyles and important beliefs for the individual, as well as aspects across the societal drivers of change identified in Task 1.2. Use your imagination (within what is relevant for use of the scenario).

Tool: **PESTEL**

PESTEL	Imagine how the events/trends identified in the PESTEL tool in Task 1.2 have developed over the next five years:
POLITICAL	
ECONOMIC	
SOCIAL	
TECHNOLOGICAL	
ENVIRONMENTAL	
LEGAL	

Scenario 1: _____

_____

_____

_____

_____

_____

Scenario 2: _____

_____

_____

_____

_____

_____

Scenario 3: _____

_____

_____

_____

_____

_____

TIP: Feel free to use any kind of materials you wish when jotting down your ideas, as the space in this booklet is limited.

STAGE 2

IDEATION

Ideation involves exploring potential solutions to meet a challenge by generating ideas. This stage involves exploring as many solutions as possible before evaluating which solutions might provide a good direction forward for the project.

TASK 2.1

IDENTIFY OPPORTUNITIES

Within the scenarios you have built, are there any challenges, opportunities or needs that emerge? What kind of challenges or threats do you see? Are the challenges you first identified the most relevant, or are there any other challenges that are more important to solve? What emerges from the context, and where could you join the dots between the person and the challenge, and offer a solution?

Specify all of the challenges and opportunities you see by writing them down.

Select one of the challenges for which it might be possible to find a solution.

Rephrase the challenge into an opportunity.

IN CASE OF EMERGENCIES: Hold a vote if you cannot come to an agreement in another way.

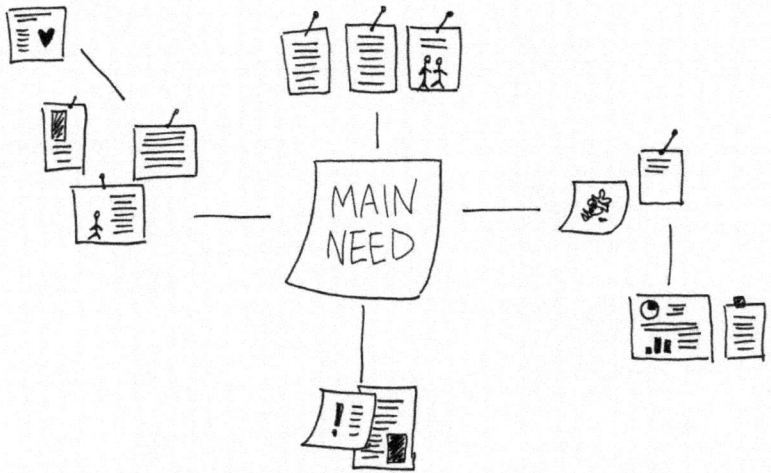

TASK 2.2

PETAL

It is time to develop ideas for future solutions (ideas for products, services etc.) that exploit the opportunity. In this task we will use the 'Petal' tool.

Start by writing down the opportunity from Task 2.1 and the name of the target person defined in Task 1.1 in the middle of the Petal tool (see next page).

Explore four different subsidiary needs to this opportunity, for example:

> **Physical needs** (food, water, etc.)
>
> **Social needs** (interaction, culture, etc.)
>
> **Ideological needs** (values, expression, etc.)
>
> **Functional needs** (improvement, problem solving, etc.)

Explore what kind of ideas that could answer these opportunities. Be as specific as possible.

Tool: **Petal**

Use the Petal tool to explore your scenario.

1. Define the targeted person and the opportunity

2. Define four subsidiary needs

3. Propose and explore ideas that meet these opportunities

TIP: Physical needs are related to the person's senses and sensorial experiences. Social needs are related to how that person relates to other people. Ideological needs are about values, and functional needs are, for example, needs that helps the person solve something or perform better.

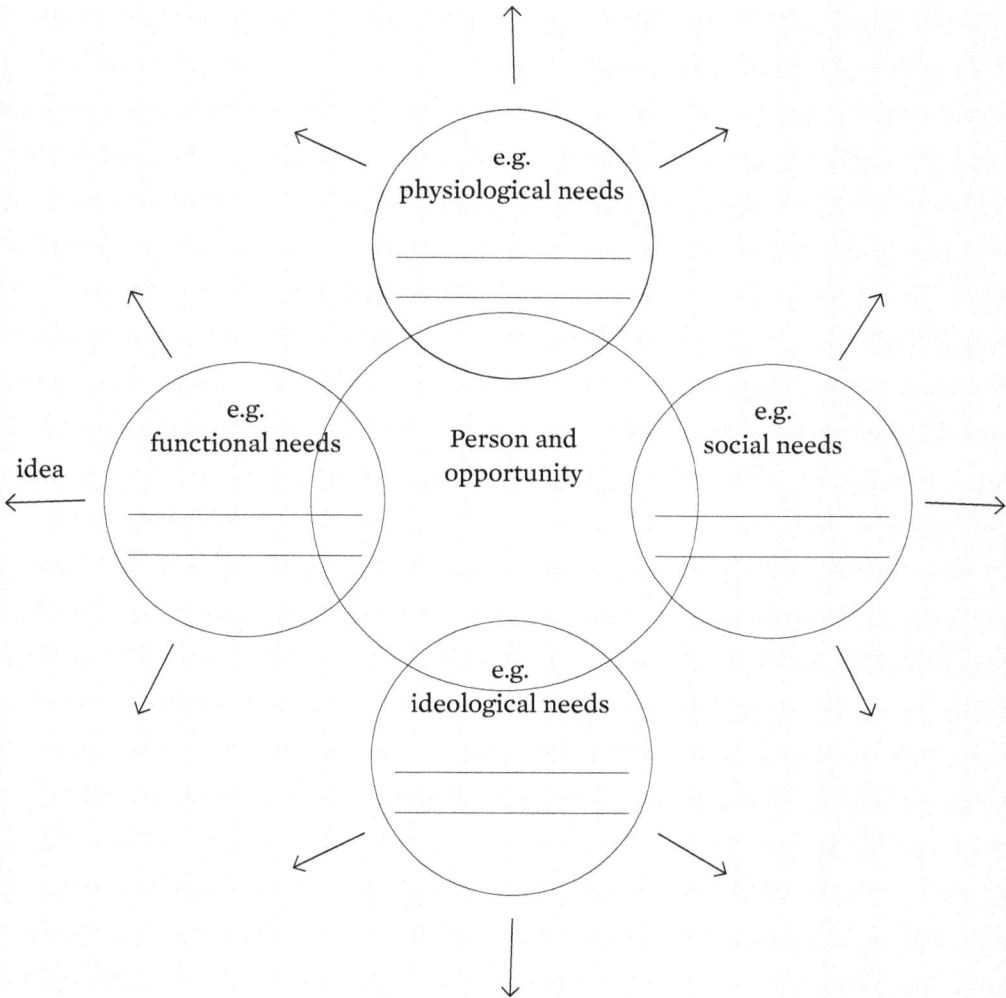

e.g.
physiological needs
_____
_____

e.g.
functional needs
_____
_____

Person and
opportunity

e.g.
social needs
_____
_____

e.g.
ideological needs
_____
_____

idea

TASK 2.3

DRAW

Select one idea each (you can select the same one if you like).

Have each member sketch the selected idea on a sheet of paper, then pass this sheet to the next person so that they can add whatever fits.

You then continue to pass the sheets around until everyone has contributed to every sheet of paper.

At the end of this session, you will have as many ideas as the number of the people in the group, so that all of you will have contributed to developing all the ideas.

TIP: This task is easiest to do if you are working in groups. If you work alone, we recommend you to select three ideas and make a drawing of each of them.

STAGE 3

CONCEPT DEVELOPMENT

Describe each idea in detail, so that they feel real.
Assess the ideas.

TASK 3.1

CREATE A CRITERIA LIST

Use the ideas developed in Tasks 2.2 and 2.3. Discuss these ideas, and comment in particular on:

> **How functional will each solution be?**
>
> **How usable will each solution be?**
>
> **How desirable will each solution be?**
>
> **How viable will each solution be?**
>
> **Which of the solutions would you spend time working on?**

From this discussion, you should develop a list of criteria, and then evaluate each idea according to those criteria. You should end up with one idea, or merge aspects of several ideas into a single idea.

> TIP: If you already know which idea you are developing, you could simplify this task by just drawing up the list of criteria.

How functional will each solution be? _____
_____
_____
_____
_____

How usable will each solution be? _____
_____
_____
_____
_____

How desirable will each solution be? _____
_____
_____
_____
_____

How viable will each solution be?_____
_____
_____
_____
_____

Which of the solutions would you spend time working on?
_____
_____
_____
_____

Criteria list:

_____

_____

_____

_____

_____

_____

_____

_____

_____

_____

_____

_____

_____

_____

_____

_____

_____

_____

_____

_____

_____

_____

_____

_____

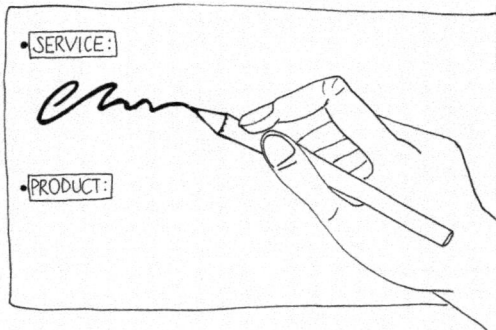

TASK 3.2

DEFINE AND CLARIFY

Make the idea as realistic as possible. Draw many quick sketches of what this could look like, and consider what would make this work. For a product, this might be technology and considerations around production, while for services you might need to consider the number of users and organisational aspects. As you develop the idea, it will gradually turn into a product or service concept.

TIP: Draw the product or service from different perspectives, pull out interesting details or features, and make the product and the service more and more realistic as you draw.

An interesting exercise is to try to make what you are developing into both a service and a product.

TASK 3.3

USER JOURNEY

Come back to the person defined as a user in Task 1.1, and any other users you may have identified during the development of the concept.

Discuss how you would like your user(s) to experience the concept defined in Task 3.2.

Draw a step-by-step user journey.

TIP: This exercise forces you to see your idea through the eyes of the user. Depending on the user's past experience, the service or product may vary. You could develop several potential user journeys.

---

notice   *attract*   *decide/*
                                                          buy

---

TIP: Be specific, and include at least five stages of the product or service use. The concept will most likely have over 50 potential stages (from long before the user knows about the product or service until long after the use has taken place).

Tool: **User journey**
The user journey encompasses all of the activities that take place before the user knows about the product/service, until the moment they are aware of the product/service, when they have bought or started using the product service, when the product/service is delivered, and experiences through use and after use of the product/service.

receive   *use*   *dispose*

STAGE 4
PROTOTYPING

Make the concept as real and alive as possible by
creating a prototype.

TASK 4.1

PLAN YOUR PROTOTYPE

By now, you should have a good enough understanding of your concept to enable you to design a prototype to test your idea. The prototype can be a physical model, a process, an enactment, a workshop, or take another form.

On the next page, some relevant questions are asked that can help you get started.

> TIP: At this stage, it is recommended to have some rough prototypes before spending a lot of time developing a fully functional model or approach.

Which part(s) of the concept would you like to prototype?

_____

_____

_____

What kind of resources do you have (paper, clay, textiles, people, rooms etc.)?_____

_____

_____

_____

What would you like to achieve by prototyping your concept?

_____

_____

_____

How realistically possible is it to create your prototype?_____

_____

_____

_____

How could you use information from prototyping to redesign your concept? _____

_____

_____

_____

TIP: The test should consider that what is being developed is at the sketch level. This will affect the input you receive. Consider how you may get the input you need to develop the concept further.

TASK 4.2

TEST AND EVALUATE

Test the feasibility of your prototype by comparing and evaluating it against the criteria you defined in Task 3.1. Make the test and evaluation as realistic as possible in order to get valuable input.

Discuss which presumptions you have about the concept that are important to have confirmed or disproved.

Test the concept, both in the workshop and also outside it with people you have in mind who could be target customers or have a stake in what you are developing.

In this phase, it is also important to look outside to see whether you have any competitors or whether there are any organisations you could learn from.

TASK 4.3

REDESIGN AND IMPLEMENT

Use the findings from the test and evaluation in Task 4.2 to improve and redesign the concept.

Remember that it can take time to develop an adequate solution. Every step will therefore provide useful information that may be used in the preparations.

If you have developed something you are satisfied with, you may consider going forward with the concept.

This is the last step in this step-by-step process. If you have completed all the 11 previous tasks, you will now have reached the goal of the learning exercise.

HUZZAH! Congratulations for a well-performed design thinking process! We hope you have had an interesting experience.

DIPLOMA

AWARDED TO

_____

for completion of a design thinking workshop.
Project title:

_____

Date:

_____

Design thinking is a holistic approach to development work, where the desire for continuous improvement and learning is a significant attitude. People are put at the centre of attention.*

---

*Inspired by Herbert Simon's expression that design is 'how things ought to be' (1994 [1969]).

THOUGHTS ON THE PROCESS

How the step-by-step process relates to a general design process.

In this chapter, we will provide reflections on how these different stages relate to a general design process, and what you might want to think about when developing products or services.

Similar to a design process, the step-by-step process is prepared in several stages. A design process often starts with a research stage, with the goal of understanding the context of the challenge at hand. When an overview of the challenge has been established, the challenge is redefined and the process evolves into an ideation stage. In this stage, one or more concepts are selected for further testing and concept development. In the final stage, the concept is implemented and evaluated.

In a real-life process, the stages would be less linear and less bounded by start and finish, and one might go back and forth between the stages. An experienced designer would develop what needs to be done while learning about the context and what is being developed, as well as about the persons who are part of the context and about what is being developed.

Immersion

The starting point in this process is to create a scenario. In a design project, the first stage would also include a large amount of research. One often seeks to understand the persons who are part of the context and/or the technology available. In a design process, research is important to identify facts and figures, but also in order to find inspiration. It consists of structured data collection, sampling and exploration. It also consists of a sensory exploration of the area, the challenges or the materials. The research that needs to be conducted in this phase has to be broad in order to allow the designer to investigate areas that may not appear strictly relevant initially, but may yield more interesting insights as the project progresses.

Later in the process, when the concept is defined further, there will be more systematic research into key areas, which for a physical product would involve materials, technology or a deeper immersion into the users' context. However, it is important not to let this hinder the process by emphasising the analytical aspects and strict limitation to collection of data. A sensory exploration of the context is important so that unexpected changes and innovative solutions are allowed to surface. It is just as important to identify the absence of research or products, and to explore why no one has looked at these challenges before.

Ideation

In this stage, the participants explore different opportunities identified, and potential solutions to make full use of these. The Petal tool is a semi-structured approach to idea-generation. It allows the participants to explore various solutions.

The ideation stage will always include some form of brainstorming, either by yourself or in a group. An important aspect to remember in brainstorming is not to critique or focus early on, but to open the discussion up to a range of different solutions. This technique is also a method to get rid of clichés and to explore other solutions. Through an interchange between ideation alone and in groups, will it be possible to drive the process forward, and at the same time create ownership in the group of what is developed. This stage of ideation can be described by a 'Yes, and ...' (rather than 'No, but ...') attitude, where the goal is to develop as many ideas as possible and to build upon all of the ideas you produce collectively. An important factor in exploring many different solutions in the ideation stage is to avoid bias or having a 'darling' among the suggested ideas. As soon as the teams have come up with a range of ideas, these can be evaluated and fleshed out in greater detail. An important part of ideation is to allow time for incubation, where the ideas can mature.

Concept development

In further development, critique and questioning the ideas is important to develop them into robust and viable concepts. This stage of the ideas can be described as the 'Yes, but ...' attitude. Critiquing is as important a part of the concept development stage as high-flying thinking. The expert will master both modes and treat them with equal importance.

Concept development will include detailed definition of what the idea is about. It will develop the project from something that is loosely defined to a concept that is as real as possible. During this process, a range of important decisions are made that shape the direction of the project.

Many people seem to believe that this is where the design process starts, but as this process suggests, in fact it is the middle (and here, third) stage.

In the process outlined in this booklet, this stage includes exploring the concept both as a service and a product in order to investigate the potential of the idea. Most companies and their offerings will have both a service and a product component. Flying may be a service, but many products are necessary to make it possible. The same can apply to products – perhaps focusing on the service component of what is offered will make a product stand out. Another important element in this process is the 'reduce' phase – this is the phase in a design process that will take most time. It will most likely include hours of development to get to the core of the idea. In the concept development stage, the designer will often need to conduct a second phase of research and also develop new ideas based on this. This research will identify the information that is needed in order to select the right materials, technology etc.

Prototyping

Prototyping can play a significant role in both ideation and concept development. We have defined it as a stage in itself in order to ensure this activity gets the attention it deserves.

The prototyping stage is also part of developing the concept. The prototype allows the team to explore a tangible version of what it is developing. This is a crucial point, because it allows the designer to look at the product in its correct dimensions and from all angles. This is also an important stage when developing a service, as it will make an intangible concept come alive. One approach often used is to simulate the service using role-play. Depending on the budget, professional actors may be brought in.

An important part of prototyping is to get real insights about how the concept will work before investing time and resources in pushing it out into the real world.

WHAT IS DESIGN THINKING?

An academic reflection on the concept of design thinking.

'Design thinking' is a complex term that is changing. It is not feasible to come up with one simple definition to encompass all of what design thinking is – nor is it desirable. We emphasise the following:

> *Design thinking is a holistic approach to development work, where the desire for continuous improvement and learning is a significant attitude. People are at the centre of attention.*

> *Design thinking is reflection through action. This means that the approach and solution to the challenge emerges while working.*

> *Design thinking combines analytical and intuitive mindsets and allows the involvement of all stakeholders in a co-operative activity. The aim of this co-operation is to provide a joint journey towards a solid solution.*

The first quote above is our own definition, including an attitude that influences how we think and that commits us to a continuous improvement and learning process. The people one develops the solution for will be an important motivation and inspiration for the development work. This definition is inspired by the American social scientist, computer scientist and recipient of the Nobel Prize in Economics Herbert Simon's definition that 'the designer is concerned with how things ought to be' (1994 [1969]).

The second quote, 'Design thinking is reflection through action', is our interpretation of the American philosopher and organisational learning researcher Donald Schön's observations of how designers go about their work (2011 [1959]). He observed designers working to build prototypes, and while they were building them, their understanding of the challenge they were working on grew. The design process forced the designers to make decisions while building the prototype, and the committing nature of these decisions facilitated progress on the work.

The third quote, 'Design thinking combines analytical and intuitive mindsets', is inspired by the Canadian economist and strategy researcher Roger Martin's definition of design thinking (2009). He states that there are two schools of thought in creativity. One is the analytic school, which relies on analysis and rigid structures to develop ideas. The other is intuitive, relying on gut feelings and making decisions without rationalising first. According to Professor Martin, design thinking combines these schools.

In addition, we would like to expand this by adding the collaborative effort that is the modern design process. An important part of this process is a desire to come up with a strong idea or concept that drives the process of development. Without this, what is developed will not be recognised as 'design' work – or at least not good design work.

What the three sources of inspiration above have in common is that design is about development and process. The difference from other innovation and management processes is that design does not follow a set procedure, but changes depending on the context one works in. This constant change is a significant part of design thinking, and part of understanding design thinking is perhaps to accept that it will not be properly defined or learned through a simple method. However, it can be experienced, and by practice be learned.

The approach in this booklet, therefore, is to make design thinking more concrete by introducing it through a step-by-step process that follows guiding principles, mirroring a generic design process.

DESIGN PRINCIPLES

Design thinking is built on several principles. The design researcher Dr Monika Hestad (co-author of this booklet), with the design and innovation researcher and philosopher Dr Jamie Brassett, surveyed significant design literature and practices looking for the drivers of design thinking (Hestad and Brasset, 2013). They came up with principles that cover the breadth of what design thinking is. These have been further developed into ten principles by teaching and in practice. These are powerful principles, and when starting to master them, you move beyond the buzz of design thinking to become a design thinker yourself.

1. Wonder
Design often starts with wondering about something, a matter that concerns you (Martin, 2009). Before coming up with the idea that points to a solution, we often start with a question. This could be 'What will the world look like ten years from now?' – a big question for which there cannot be a precise answer. But as

soon as you have asked the question, you can unfetter your mind and imagine what the world could be like.

2. Learn about the context
In order to 'join the dots', the designer will have to understand the context the problem is part of. If it is a service that is being developed, the context could involve the company or organisation's heritage, culture, brand or products. It could be about the market, with its suppliers, competitors and customers. And it could be about 'drivers of change' in society, such as political, economic, social, demographic, technological, environmental, legal or other changes. Research is not merely something that starts the process, but it is an activity throughout the process.

3. Identify value
Businesses and organisations are there for a reason. The reason why we buy into a product or service is that it brings us something of value. In design vocabulary, looking at what users need or desire is often a goal. 'Need' in design is not as concrete as 'I need a mobile phone.' It goes deeper than that. It involves tapping into inner desires. The mobile phone, for example, meets the needs of practical communication and social interaction, but it can also be a tool to provide a feeling of security or a means of expressing your identity. By understanding the underlying reasons that drive behaviours, it is possible to propose new concepts that can create new needs and demands.

4. Zoom in and out
In design, it is important to have a narrow, detailed focus on the task at hand, while at the same time seeing the bigger picture. This is a vital balance throughout the journey. When you have designed a product, service or even a business model, both the

minor details and the bigger picture are important. It is important to allow yourself to take a step back to look at what you have developed, both from your own individual perception and from other people's insights about the world. Design is part of a context, and will therefore always need to explore and learn more about the context. Zooming in and out is an important part of constantly engaging with what you are developing, and seeing what you are developing in light of the bigger picture.

5. Diverge and converge

When developing solutions, the process includes both divergent stages, where it is about opening up and exploring, and convergent stages, where the aim is to join all the dots together (Gray et al., 2010). In the divergent stage, you seek different forms of input. The aim of these stages is to explore as many concepts as possible; it is about listening and building upon each other's ideas. When we start to evaluate and decide which idea we will go forward with, we close the session and move into a convergent stage. The aim then is to narrow the focus and develop the ideas by critiquing them. In this phase, we seek to come up with a rational solution for the concept. The divergent/convergent process applies not only in the ideation stage, but throughout the process in order to explore the concept that is being developed.

6. Iterate and reduce

Iteration is the act of repeating a process with the aim of coming closer to the core of the challenge and learning about it. Once the core idea has been defined, the design team will find themselves developing the same sketch over and over again. In every drawing, something is explored and the designer moves closer to a solution. The design agenda often includes a quest for simplicity. This means that the main concept will be worked on over and over again to make it as simple and easily accessible as possible.

7. Integrate people's views

Empathy is important when designing the solution, as it will normally be used by someone other than the design team. Designers seek to observe the product or service through the eyes of different actors involved. This could be the user, the customer, the service provider or anybody else who has a stake in the product or the service. Empathy can be difficult without having experienced challenges yourself. It would therefore be beneficial for the developers to have these experiences themselves, but this will not necessarily be possible. In the development process, it is important to seek input from various stakeholders and obtain input from users and the social context as early as possible.

8. Include both analysis and intuitive reasoning

Multiple decisions are made when designing. This means that the reasoning will be intuitive as well as analytical (Martin, 2009). In the design process, it is important to develop a list of criteria the design should meet. This starts at the outset of the process with developing a project brief. The more you learn about the concept and the context you are designing for, the more detailed it is possible to make this criteria list.

The list of criteria often has four key themes (The Helen Hamlyn Centre for Design):

Usability – how easy it is to use, and whether there are any unique user scenarios that need to be taken into consideration.
Desirability – how desirable the concept is, which may include aesthetic considerations or the overall experience.
Viability – how feasible it is to produce the solution, and how

well the solution will meet specific concerns regarding delivery or the business model.

Functionality – what the functions are, and how the solution will facilitate them.

9. Visualise and prototype

Visualisation serves multiple purposes in developing ideas. Initially, visualisation is a way of thinking while developing. The designer can start with a rough idea or thought, and then use sketching to develop this further. Visualisation is also a medium for communicating and sharing ideas. This is of particular importance when collaborating in groups. The members of the group will find that by visualising the idea through drawing, they grow a shared vision of what they are developing. Many fear that they will not be able to visualise their idea properly because they lack training in drawing. One way to overcome this could be to cut out pictures from magazines and create a collage of the concept, or just accept that it is not the beauty of the drawing that is important, but rather that everyone involved understands the idea that has been expressed.

Designers use prototypes as a tool to test ideas. In the beginning of the design process, it is possible to develop early physical models that serve as sketches. These rough prototypes or mock-ups can be built quickly to develop an idea the designers want to test as part of – or even the whole of – the concept. When making prototypes, the designer will have to make choices. Prototyping is not limited to physical products, but can also be used for services.

For services, a 'pilot' will be a form of prototype. Here, different stakeholders' roles can be acted out or simulated in order to learn about the use of the service.

10. Stay optimistic

Problems rarely have a single solution – quite often, they have many. This optimistic attitude to finding solutions is key in a development process. Using trial and error, working can also be interesting and fun. During the process, it is also important to allow yourself breaks. A long walk or doing chores may be just what you need in order to let your subconscious work with the idea.

The step-by-step process and the principles in this booklet have been developed to provide a taste of what design thinking can do for managers. Donald Schön introduced the idea that managers should learn from this approach as early as 1959. Almost sixty years later, his thoughts remain relevant.

We encourage you who test the process to gradually adapt it to your own business or organisation, and to start to use the principles in your everyday work. Through embracing a mindset with people at the centre and a desire for continuous improvement and learning, as well as an exploration of the principles, you can go deeper into what design thinking is about. You will then also experience how designers' mindset develops both sustainable organisations and meaningful products and services.

HELPDESK

Reference list, recommended additional resources and tools.

Design and design thinking is a blossoming field, and a wide range of resources are available. Below are a few titles that have inspired us when developing this booklet. These include works by academics and practitioners who are recognised as thought leaders within design thinking and within the design field. The design thinking references include advocates for the field, critical voices and historic perspectives. We also include three classic publications on design which have been found particularly helpful in understanding how designers think and work. The resources labelled 'toolkits' are handy books that provide a large variety of tools which could be introduced at the different stages.

Design and Design thinking

Abbing, R. Eric (2010) *Brand-driven Innovation: Strategies for Development and Design.* London: Ava Publishing.

Brown, Tim (2008, June). Design Thinking. *Harvard Business Review*, 84–92.

Brown, Tim and Wyatt, Jocelyn (2010, Winter). Design Thinking for Social Innovation. *Stanford Social Innovation Review*. Retrieved February 27, 2017, from http://ssir.org/articles/entry/design_thinking_for_social_innovation.

Cisco (2016, June 02). The Zettabyte Era – Trends and Analysis – Cisco. San Francisco, *CA: Cisco Systems*, Inc. Retrieved February 27, 2017, from www.cisco.com/c/en/us/solutions/collateral/service-provider/visual-networking-index-vni/vni-hyperconnectivity-wp.html.

Cross, Nigel (2006). *Designerly Ways of Knowing*. London: Springer-Verlag.

Dorst, Kees (2003). *Understanding Design: 150 Reflections on Being a Designer*. Amsterdam: BIS Publishers.

Farstad, Per and Jevnaker, Birgit Helene (2010) *Design i praksis: Designledelse og innovasjon*. Oslo: Universitetsforlaget. [In Norwegian].

HBR (2015, September). Spotlight Section 'The Evolution in Design Thinking', *Harvard Business Review*. Retrieved February 27, 2017, from https://hbr.org/2015/09/design-thinking-comes-of-age.

Hestad, Monika and Brassett, Jamie (2013, May 14–17). Teaching 'Design Thinking' in the Context of Innovation Management – From Process to a Dialogue about Principles. Conference paper at *DRS // CUMULUS Oslo 2013 – The 2nd International Conference for Design Education Researchers, Oslo*.

Jordan, Patrick (2000). *Designing Pleasurable Products: An Introduction to the New Human Factors*. London: Taylor & Francis.

Kimbell, Lucy (2011). Rethinking Design Thinking: Part I. *Design and Culture*, 3(3), 285–306. Retrieved February 27,

2017, from www.tandfonline.com/doi/abs/10.2752/1754708 11X13071166525216.

Kimbell, Lucy (2012). Rethinking Design Thinking: Part II. *Design and Culture,* 4(2), 129–148. Retrieved February 27, 2017, from www.tandfonline.com/doi/pdf/10.2752/1754708 12X13281948975413.

Lawson, Bryan (1997). *How Designers Think: The Design Process Demystified.* Oxford: Architectural Press.

Liedtka, Jeanne, King, Andrew and Bennett, Kevin (2013). *Solving Problems with Design Thinking.* New York: Columbia Business School.

Lockwood, Thomas, ed. (2010). *Design Thinking: Integrating Innovation, Customer Experience, and Brand Value.* New York: Allworth Press.

Martin, Roger (2009). *The Design of Business: Why Design Thinking Is the Next Competitive Advantage.* Boston, MA: Harvard Business Press.

McCullagh, Kevin (2010, March 29). Design Thinking: Everywhere and Nowhere, Reflections on The Big Re-think. *Core77.* Retrieved February 27, 2017, from www.core77.com/blog/featured_items/design_thinkingeverywhere_and_nowhere_reflections_on_the_big_re-think__16277.asp.

Mulgan, Geoff (2014, January 08). Design in Public and Social Innovation. *Nesta.* Retrieved February 27, 2017, from www.nesta.org.uk/publications/design-public-and-social-innovation.

Neumeier, Martin (2009). *The Designful Company: How to Build a Culture of Nonstop Innovation.* Berkeley, CA: New Riders.

Norman, Donald and Verganti, Robert (2014). Incremental and Radical Innovation: Design Research vs. Technology and Meaning Change. *Design Issues,* 30(1), 78–96.

Schön, Donald (2011 [1959]). *The Reflective Practitioner.* Farnham: Ashgate.

Simon, Herbert A. (1994 [1969]) *The Sciences of the Artificial.* 2nd ed. Cambridge, MA: The MIT Press.

Stamm, Bettina von (2008). *Managing Innovation, Design and Creativity.* London: Wiley.

Tovey, Mikey (2009). The Passport to Practice. In S. Garner & Chris Evans (Eds.), *Design and Designing: A Critical Introduction* (82–96). London: Berg.

Verganti, Roberto (2009). *Design-Driven Innovation. Changing the Rules of Competition by Radically Innovating What Things Mean.* Boston, MA: Harvard Business Press.

Toolkits

Gray, Dave, Brown, Sunny and Macanufo, James (2010). *Game Storming: A Playbook for Innovators, Rulebreakers and Changemakers.* Cambridge: O'Reilly Media.

Silverstein, David, Samuel, Philip and DeCarlo, Neil (2009). *The Innovator's Toolkit: 50+ Techniques for Predictable and Sustainable Organic Growth.* Hoboken, NJ: John Wiley & Sons..

Sims, Nikki Highmore (2006). *How to Run a Great Workshop*. Harlow: Pearsons.

Stickdorn, Marc and Schneider, Jakob (2010). *This is Service Design Thinking: Basics – Tools – Cases*. Amsterdam: BIS Publishers.

Online resource pages

All online resources referred to in this booklet were retrieved on February 27, 2017. If the resources have moved, we recommend you search online for the details listed in the reference.

Templates for all of the tools suggested in this step-by-step process can be found at www.brandvalley.co.uk/resources

Overview of various toolkits
https://mappingsocialdesign.wordpress.com/2013/11/19/mapping-social-design-practice-beyond-the-toolkit/

Arup Foresight Drivers of Change
http://www.driversofchange.com/tools/

British Design Council
www.designcouncil.org.uk
www.designcouncil.org.uk/news-opinion/design-process-what-double-diamond

Core 77 (design magazine and resources)
www.core77.com

Design Management Institute
www.dmi.org

Design Thinking for Educators
https://designthinkingforeducators.com

Harvard Business Review
https://hbr.org
https://hbr.org/video/4443548301001/the-explainer-de-sign-thinking

Ideo.org resource page
www.designkit.org/methods

Ken Robinson (2006), 'Do Schools Kill Creativity?', TED Talks
www.ted.com/talks/ken_robinson_says_schools_kill_creativity

Learning Graphic Facilitation (Biggerpicture.dk)
https://www.youtube.com/watch?v=S5DJC6LaOCI

Lucy Kimbell and Joe Julier, The Social Design Methods Menu: In Perpetual Beta
www.lucykimbell.com/stuff/Fieldstudio_SocialDesignMethods-Menu.pdf

Method Cards for IDEO
www.ideo.com/work/method-cards/

The Helen Hamlyn Centre for Design
www.hhc.rca.ac.uk
www.inclusivedesigntoolkit.com/betterdesign2/whatis/whatis.html

THE TEAM BEHIND THIS BOOKLET

Dr Monika Hestad - Founder, author and concept developer
Monika is the founder of Brand Valley, and has worked in industrial design and business innovation for more than a decade. Her role in this booklet was to design the overall concept, lead the project, write the text and facilitate delivery of the process. In addition to working at Brand Valley, she also lectures at Central Saint Martins, University of the Arts London. She regularly provides business audiences in Europe with insights into design, branding and innovation. Monika has a Master's degree in Industrial Design and a PhD in Industrial Design and Branding from Oslo School of Architecture and Design. She is author of the bestselling book *Branding and Product Design: An Integrated Perspective* (2013, published by Gower in the UK and Ashgate in the US; since 2016, published by Routledge).

Anders Groenli- Author and production editor
Anders is a co-founder of Brand Valley, and has been responsible for the production editing of this booklet and providing concept development advice from a non-designer's perspective. He is a political scientist with a background in consulting, government and politics. Anders currently works in strategic security risk management. He has an MSc in Global Security from Cranfield

University at the Defence Academy of the United Kingdom and a BA in Organisational Psychology and Political Science from the University of Oslo.

Silvia Rigoni – Author, illustrator and concept developer
Silvia became part of the team behind the booklet in the autumn of 2012. She has been involved in developing the concept for both the workshop and this booklet, illustrating the tasks and also delivering the workshop at the Innovation Leadership Forum. Silvia's background is a mix of product design, project management and innovation management. Her passion and field of speciality is food innovation. She has a BA in Industrial Design from Istituto Europeo di Design in Rome and a Master's degree in Innovation Management from Central Saint Martins, University of the Arts London.

Dr Ingvild Digranes - Scientific editor
Ingvild's background is in art and design education, and she is currently an Associate Professor at the Oslo and Akershus University College of Applied Sciences in Norway. She teaches educational theory, learning theories and methods in specialised courses for designers, architects and artists who want to qualify for a career in education. Ingvild has a PhD in Art and Design Education from the Oslo School of Architecture and Design.

Dr Bettina von Stamm - Guest contributor
Bettina has focused on understanding and enabling innovation since 1992. She shares insights and learnings from her journey through her company, the Innovation Leadership Forum, and is increasingly convinced that the context of the twenty-first century demands that we embrace the triple bottom line – Planet,

People, Profit – as the starting point for any innovation. In addition to being a sought-after inspirational speaker around the world, she has authored the books *The Future of Innovation Paperback* (with Anna Trifilova, Gower, 2009), *Managing Innovation, Design and Creativity* (Wiley, 2008) and *The Innovation Wave: Addressing Future Challenges: Meeting the Corporate Challenge* (Wiley, 2002). Bettina trained as an architect at the Christian-Albrechts-Universität zu Kiel, has an MBA and PhD in design management from the London Business School (the latter with the title *The Impact of Context and Complexity in New Product Development*).

BRAND VALLEY PUBLICATIONS

Brand Valley's work is based on more than a decade of research in branding, design and innovation, with a continuous motivation to develop and share knowledge across these disciplines. The aim of the booklets is to enable and empower companies within the new economy. The philosophy behind these is a belief that people respond to businesses that are creative, integrated, value-centred, reflective and sustainable.

All of the booklets are collaborative projects between Brand Valley and partners in academia or other consultancies.

Brand Valley Publications is the publication arm of Brand Valley Design Ltd (UK) and Brand Valley AS (Norway).

www.brandvalley.co.uk
publications@brandvalley.co.uk
Facebook: @BrandValley
Twitter: @brandval

ACKNOWLEDGEMENTS

The authors would like to thank Dr Bettina von Stamm for engaging us to deliver the process in the 7th Innovation Leadership Experienced Event of the Innovation Leadership Forum Networking Group, workshop participants for their valuable input, and the students on the MA Innovation Management course at Central Saint Martins (CSM) and the short course, 'Business Design'. We would like to thank Dr Jamie Brassett at CSM for pushing our thinking. We would also like to thank our dear colleagues at Brand Valley, Marianne Lydersen, Hans Martin Erlandsen and Ihna Stallemo, for encouragement as well as suggestions for how to improve the booklet. The authors would also like to thank Huw Jones of Cove Publishing Support Services for proofreading the manuscript for this booklet. Finally, we would like to thank Ingrid Grønli for feeding hungry authors.

www.ingramcontent.com/pod-product-compliance
Lightning Source LLC
Chambersburg PA
CBHW041217030426
42336CB00023B/3370